Moments In Time

By
Gil Saenz

Illustrations by

George Perazza

For all my relatives, friends,
and co-workers who have continued
to be such a strong source
of support and encouragement.

MOMENTS IN TIME
By Gil Saenz © Copyright 1995

ISBN 0-9635681-4-0

Preface

Sometimes there are moments in a person's life which may be so unusual or unique that the person may wish very strongly to preserve, maintain, and treasure them in a special way. This is an area where poetry can help. The metaphorical and symbolic language of poetry is able to describe all the emotion and experience that is usually associated with such moments. It is able to come close to telling what actually took place and what really happened.

Special moments such as these may only last a very short while in reality: a few minutes, or an hour. However, the experience has such a profound impact that the time span actually seems much longer in a person's memory. The person is able to recall every detail.

As you will note the following forty poems which have been previously published in other places as well are placed into four categories: Moments 1) In Reflection, 2) In Nature, 3) In Romance, and 4) In the Spiritual. This is done more for ease of understanding and recognition. I hope that you will be able to identify with and appreciate some of my "Moments In Time" that are described here.

Gil Saenz
July, 1994

Table of Contents

Table of Contents (continued)

I. Moments in Reflection

Moments in Time

The many good things we remember,
Many brief and fleeting hours,
Special times in all our lives,
As bright as the Spring flowers

Charming periods that we cherish,
Making us who and what we are,
Filled with excitement and/or calm,
All grown rosy and better from afar.

They are parts of our personal being
From childhood to adulthood years,
Leaving on us an indelible mark,
Even as their memory begins to disappear.

Summer, Fall, Winter, and Spring,
The four seasons have their own
Rhythm and rhyme,
They always remind us of all those
Particular moments in time.

When Paths Cross

Our eye contact reminds us
Of the secret struggles
We experience
Within our souls.

Serious thoughts reflected
Upon our faces demonstrate
The unspoken conflicts
That we are living.

Morning, noon, and nighttime,
We go through an ordinary day,
We meet our fellow travelers
Who are also attempting
The pursuit of their
Own unique way.

A casual word, a glance,
Or even a smile,
Manifests the hidden, underlying,
Personal drama unfolding;
All the yearning and striving,
Achieving our uncertain destinies.

Considering

When considering how the time goes by,
Life can be compared with a ship,
A ship with its sails flying high.
We can come along for the ride,
Or just watch as it passes by.
Most of us do both at different
Times of our lives.
Sailing along now active, now passive,
As time seems to fly by.
Trying to understand the abundance
Of mystery that we encounter,
Chasing after the treasures
And the dreams in which we believe,
Sailing along in the sea of time.

Courage

Dare to follow your heart's desire.
Life, after all, never asks of us
Any more than that which is required.
Don't be discouraged if things don't always
Turn out just so.
Sometimes our mistakes are just as important
As the things we already know.
Never lose sight of your final goal.
Remember the parts are also just as important
As the whole.
Courage is something we all must maintain.
We must always be willing to pick up
And keep going again.

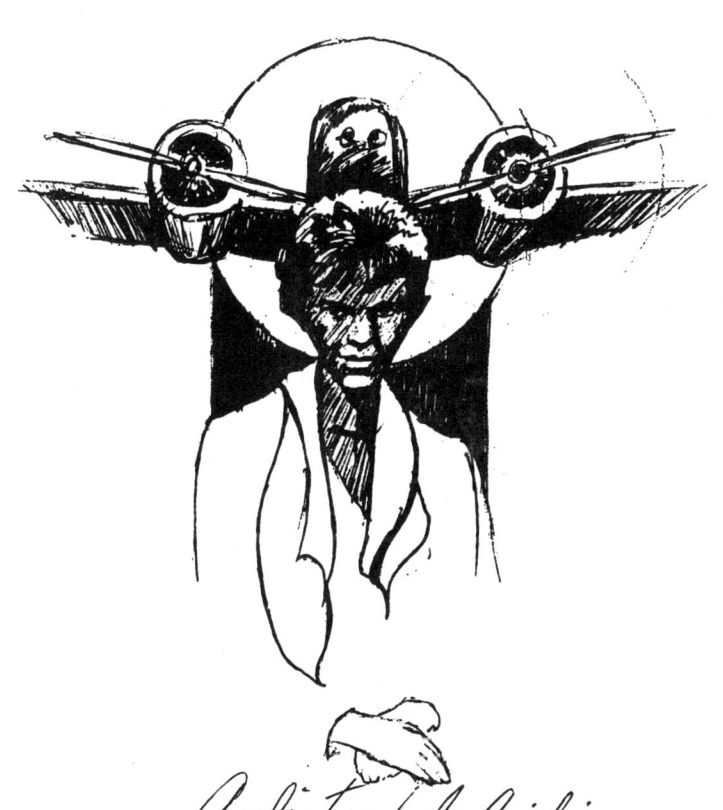

Amelia Earhart - Aviatrix

A Thought

A thought can do many things.
A notion, a wish, or a feeling
Can build huge bridges,
Fly large jet planes,
Create beautiful works of art,
Make intricate machines
That calculate faster
Than the human mind.
A thought can write a song
From a pleasant memory,
Or it can create a rainbow
On a plain canvas.
A thought can discover
Fresh marvels and wonders
In each passing day.

Edison

Peak Moments

Without a care for time,
It becomes trivial sometimes.
It no longer matters,
It is unimportant,
Irrelevant.
The mystic knows the feeling well.
For those who are so absorbed
In their own activity,
Their sense of time falls
By the wayside,
And is forgotten.
Another peak moment
Has now come and gone.

Computer Generation

Computer generation,
It is filled with much sophistication.
Bits, bytes, programs, and concatenations,
Facts, figures, database, trends, online reports,
They're all the latest business field sensation.
It's not the answer to all our problems,
But it has entered all facets of our daily lives,
It has so many different kinds of applications.
It has even begun to decipher the genetic code,
To unlock some of life's mysteries,
Much to many people's alarm and consternation.
While it has created the loss of many jobs
Which were menial, repetitious, and boring,
It has created a large new industry of jobs
Which are computer related, highly technical,
And leave room for much exploring.
Computer generation,
It has created a quiet revolution,
And it has completely modernized our nation.

Poetry Man

Poetry man your destiny has already been ordained.
You were meant to be a teacher,
A lover of words,
A consummate storyteller,
Both otherworldly and mundane,
A lover of the artful phrase,
An entertainer with wit and charm,
Simple and yet urbane.
You must give the impression
Of a sophisticated, self-possessed man,
Who has become wise to the ways
Of the world since time began.
You must be all to each and each to all,
Pleasing most as you compose.
After all, poetry is very different from prose.

Compassion

Listening with a patient and tender
Frame of mind,
Imagining the resulting good and evil,
And acts benign.
Feeling the same and in parallel
With the other in time,
Feeling the highs and lows
And the in-betweens,
The shame and pride.
Identifying with the other
In such a way
That a sympathetic understanding
Would always hold sway.

World Traveler

I have known the wonders of life,
The beauty of the music,
Of the day and the night,
As they would go rushing by.

I have seen the heavens
From both near and far,
Traveling hundreds of miles
By jet plane per hour.
I could look out the window
Of the huge airplane
And survey the vast expanse
Of blue sky and endless terrain.

I have journeyed far from home,
Even to Africa and beyond.
Seeing different peoples, places,
And customs was a privilege
And a gift that I would
Always reflect fondly upon.

II. Moments in Nature

Weeping Willow

Tall weeping willow tree,
Offering your light green shade
From the afternoon sun,
Your many outstretched branches,
And narrow thin leaves
Are all peacefully, and restfully
Posing in attitude of calmness,
Your beauty and tranquility
Provide for quiet reflection
And restfulness
For all those who walk by.

Sparkling Raindrops

As the raindrops descended
Upon my car's window, one by one,
The little bubbles that they formed
Were shiny and glistening like the sun.

Their restful rhythm and harmless patter,
Bestowed a sense of calm,
And a feeling that
Nothing else ever really mattered.

The little silver streaming columns
Of each droplet coming down,
Produced a special feeling
Of the harmony of nature,
That was somehow present all around.

Impressions

Orange, yellow, gold, green, red,
Blue, white, and brown
Are some of the lively colors
That are present in the natural
Scene all around.

A profusion of shades and hues
Are readily available in the sky
With its wondrous patterns of clouds,
Or its many sunrisings and sunsets
That regularly please our eye.

Cool and gentle breezes blowing
Softly in the summertime,
Make the leaves in the trees,
A flickering green and white light
As they toss back and forth
Effortlessly keeping rhythmical time.

Leaves and Breezes

The various kinds of trees
All stood quietly
With grace and dignity.
The neatly mowed lawn
Resembled a matted green carpet
Spread out among all the trees.
The occasional breezes
Blew the larger leaves
Slowly back and forth.
Whole sets of branches moved
And swayed in unison
As if all joined together.
Meanwhile, small spots of sunlight
Filtered through the numerous
Patterns of blowing leaves
And branches. The singing birds
Flying low with the varied shades
Of greens and browns
Blended agreeably with the other
Natural colors all around.

Sunset Mood

I saw the afterglow
Of the sunset, last night.
It was flaming orange, and red,
Golden and white.

It made me think
Of many different things,
Of how time goes on,
And of what it may sometimes bring.

It reminded me
Of a very small part
Of eternity,
As it streamed along
The horizon so unendingly.

Something for sure
That I would never outgrow,
Was that sight in the sky
Of the sunset's golden glow.

Summer Moon

The orange yellow moon
On that warm summer evening
Contained many secrets
And rare wisdom of ages past.

So many poets, romantics,
And songsters,
Had praised its mysterious
Beauty, their number was vast.

In the lower part
Of the eastern sky,
The large orange yellow sphere
Was full and bright,
And slowly ascending.

Gradually it traveled
Across the dark heavens,
While most of the world
Was settling in for slumber,
As their day was quietly ending.

Beautiful Flower

A rose, red and fresh,
On one green stem,
And newly cut,
Is a symbol of love
As well as all
Other signs
Of friendship
Which are shared.

Its singular beauty
Is used to communicate
That which may not
Always be expressed
With words.

Listen to the Waves

Ocean waves washing up along the shore,
The relaxing cadence and easy rhythm,
It makes us wish for more.
What are the waves telling us,
Amidst their gentle roar?
They are carrying many messages of wisdom,
Which are sometimes not so easy to ignore.
Calmness, peacefulness, all come in their time,
Along with tranquility evermore,
We need only stop and heed the messages of wisdom
That are daily washed up along the shore.

Autumn Breeze

Whisper softly, autumn breeze,
Through the rustle of the leaves,
Tell me something, if you please.

My heart has grown weary
With the passing of the years.
So, autumn breeze, lift my spirits.
Tell me some stories of my past,
With all the laughter and the tears.

Pure, fresh, light air,
And the slight coolness
That you possess.
Autumn breeze bring me hope
For a happier tomorrow,
That will also have some
Love and tenderness.

An Evening Walk

The light from the street lamp posts
Gave the grassy path a shimmering green look.
While the cool night air delivered
A fresh, healthy scent to go along.

The tall dark trees with outstretched arms.
And many small leaf covered branches,
Were visible against the dark blue expanse
Of nighttime sky.

In the surrounding setting of lush vegetation,
And the stimulation of the mild exercise
Which walking brings,
It was easier to meditate and think
Of peaceful imaginings.

III. Moments in Romance

Reverie

Will our paths ever cross again?
If so, I wonder when?
What does destiny hold in store,
If we should ever see each other once more?
Many years have already passed
Since the days of our youthful love
That we thought would always last.
Hoping against hope and dreaming
The impossible dream.
Trying to imagine what it would be like;
That first enchanted scene.
Winter, Fall, Summer and Spring,
The seasons slowly slip away,
As I continue hoping and wondering,
If we'll ever have our day.

Within the Midst

Within the midst
Of all the passing years,
Of all the people and places,
Both far and near,
Of all the Winters, Summers,
Autumns and Springs,
Of all the feelings, thoughts,
Moments, experiences, and memories
That they bring,
Their love had somehow miraculously survived.
By only looking into each other's eyes,
They realized how it was still
Very much alive.

Powder Blue

Lately my nights are very blue.
Now that I know there is someone who,
Was my sweetheart from the distant past,
And whose childish love I had held fast.

When the stars come out I look around,
Hoping to share with her this blue profound.
Instead I spend my nights the usual way,
Lying quietly waiting for the new day.

Lily white flower of our childish past,
Make the nighttime colors always last.
Blend in your fair color with my blue night,
And create for us the powder blue,
Of love's happiness and love's delight.

Maria and the Moon

It was warm that evening, and not quite June,
When Maria and I drove down by the river
To see the big, yellow, full moon.
She was talking and laughing,
Apparently in a good mood.
So too, the big, yellow moon likewise
Seemed happy and cheerful too.
The big, yellow, pale moon just suspended
In the dark nighttime sky,
Made me imagine many different,
Faraway places, times and lives.
How did this moon look over Vienna, Athens,
Or Rome?
Somehow it must be a little different than
The one Maria and I were seeing here at home.

Sweet Memory

Many golden sunsets,
Many days when skies were blue,
Many still summer evenings
And many rainy days too,

I have dreamed of a distant past.
Of being together happy and carefree,
Living only for the moment
When our whole world
Was just you and me.

So long ago,
All grown rosy with the years,
It was too good to be true,
Too wonderful to last
Even though what we felt
Was sincere.

Now it's all a beautiful memory
That never seems to go away,
A cherished part of my life
That in my mind
I must now and then replay.

Best Flower

Morning glory, oh morning glory,
Fresh as the morning dew,
Her pretty smile and youthfulness
Made me feel more youthful too.

Her simple and direct manner,
So plain and yet so true,
Gave her so much more charm
Than all the other flowers
Through and through.

Morning glory, her radiant beauty
Makes the birds sing,
And makes the pigeons coo.
I wonder if we will ever find
That special love which we
Have been earnestly seeking too.

Love's Images

Hand holding hand,
Two lovers walking in the park,
Or at the beach along the sand.
Beautiful, glowing, orange sunsets,
Sparkling vistas of exotic
Landscapes and places,
Music that somehow sounds improved,
Crowds of happy people with smiling faces,
Wine that tastes better than ever,
Secrets shared and confidences entrusted,
Happy nights of dancing for hours together,
Sweet perfume, flowers, and candlelight,
Blue skies, sunshine or clouds above,
These are some of the many
And various images of love.

Night Wish

Sweetness of my life,
Come to me tonight.
Help me rest my weariness,
Refresh me with your tenderness.
We'll talk, we'll laugh,
And be at ease.
We will relax together
And do what we please.
How simple it all seems,
And yet it's only in my dreams.
So, sweetness of my life,
Come to me tonight.
Let's create some
Beautiful memories together.

Summer Memento

I missed her on the first day of Summer,
I was afraid I might not see her again.
It would be a long hot season without her,
How I wish we could be friends.

I missed her on that first day of Summer,
I desired what she had represented,
I desired a love and a friend.

Warm Summer days and fair blue skies,
Made me stop to realize,
That the first day of Summer without her,
Was not quite as happy as it might have been.

Words of Love

Words of love,
Travel through the years,
Echoing the laughter,
Echoing the tears.

Words of love,
Counting the many measures,
Reflecting the simple joys
Reflecting the routine pleasures.

Words of love,
Recall the many enchanted hours,
Walking in the summer sunshine,
Walking in the fragrance of fresh flowers.

Words of love,
Sometimes resemble a dream,
Capturing days of rare beauty,
Capturing summer nights serene.

Words of love,
Describe two souls in love sincere,
Echoing their laughter,
Echoing their tears.

IV. Moments in the Spiritual

Brief Journey
(Religious Retreat)

Peace and stillness, surrounded by
The natural beauty of landscaped grounds,
With music of the birds singing,
Singing about their own happiness and joy

The Holy Spirit came into our hearts
And gave us the subtle knowledge
And prompting on how better to lead
Our lives and improve ourselves,
As we travel along on this
Brief spiritual journey.

One insight followed after another.
Gradually, more light was gained.
God be praised.

Grace

So many events,
So many circumstances,
So many accidents of birth,
Are all related in a common thread.
They form the myriad picture
Of the unique person
That we are,
And that we are becoming.

Meditation

Moments of peace have more meaning,
Times of stillness give one a gleaming,
A glimpse of fullness;
Blue, green, and gold thoughts, gently streaming,
Without any effort for you to hold.

More and more learning about the other side
Of yourself and of being,
A gentle flowing of all your senses
Which are sensing your foreverness,
For a little while.

Our Birthright

God draws us to Himself
Mostly in subtle kinds of ways,
Continually, He carefully guides us
Through all our earthly days.

Through the good times,
Or the bad, God gives us the grace,
To make the right decisions,
Whatever the problems we may face.

Our hearts silently yearn
For something in this life
Which we cannot attain,
Because God gives us the grace
To long for heaven, our birthright,
A state of eternal happiness,
And of God's loving reign.

Eternity

It is one of life's great mysteries,
Where the end of time and distance
Easily blend.
Eternity is forever,
It has no beginning,
It has no end.
It is the happy hunting ground,
And the heavenly paradise
Where most hope to go.
But it is only after one's death,
That one will really know.
It is more years than all the grains
Of sands on all the beaches in the world,
And it is farther in distance
Than the smallest star in the nighttime sky,
In the universe unfurled.

The Light of the World

God's love helps us live well each day.
At times, we don't fully grasp the many ways.
Everything that results in positive or good,
Is God's love working the way it should.
God's love is like the air we breathe.
It permeates all our world even though
We may not believe.
The simplest, small rewards that we enjoy
In our everyday,
Comes from God's mighty love that always
Follows us along our way.
If God would ever, even for a brief moment,
Take his love away,
We would all disappear, we would cease to exist.
All the lights would go out,
It would be a virtual doomsday.

Remembering

Remembering far back,
Once long ago,
When I was youthful,
And had a need to know:

All of life
Filled me with awe,
And I remained charmed
By all that I saw.

As I wandered along
Going here and there,
I felt deep down
That God was just
And fair.

The Journey

Many miles, many times, and many turns,
We have all travelled the highways
Where our souls have yearned.
They were pathways or roads
Which only we, ourselves, could traverse,
Some with great difficulty and much to learn;
Others with simple ease along the sojourn.
Life is a journey and we each must travel
Our own unique and separate way.
We are all on a path back to our Creator
Who had bestowed upon us
The gift of all our earthly days.

Religious Retreat

Listening to God's voice speak to us in our hearts,
Through the peaceful silence that was observed,
And to the Retreat Master's reading
Of the word and to all which it imparts,
There was a time to regroup, so to speak.
And a time to give our souls and ourselves
A spiritual tune-up, something which was unique.
Little by little, the changes came on
As if each were some old skin being shed.
One by one the changes and the new seeds
Of spiritual reflection were absorbed,
And gave us renewal and new growth.

Our True Destiny

Merciful and loving Savior, Lord Jesus,
The gate through which we all must pass
On the way to heaven;
Lord of all history,
Lord of all the universe,
Lamb of God who takest away
The sins of the world,
Redeemer of all mankind,
Give us the grace to pick up our cross,
And to follow after you,
To deny our very selves.
Lead us all to heaven, especially those
Who most need your guidance and care.

About The Artist

George Perazza is a commercial artist and has experience in graphic design, illustration, keylining; typesetting; computer graphics; consultation, watercolor paintings, and he also has extensive book and cover design experience.

It takes a special talent to be able to make illustrations that have sometimes a subtle and sometimes a fairly identifiable relationship to a particular text of poetry. Perazza's special ability is what adds the extra dimension of enjoyment and appreciation to the poetic sentiments expressed. This is the second book of poems in which Perazza has teamed up with Gil Saenz to provide an artistic interpretation to the lines of poetry, the first was COLORFUL IMPRESSIONS published in 1993.

About The Author

Gilbert Saenz (Pen name: Gil Saenz) is currently employed by the Detroit IRS Computing Center, Detroit, Michigan as a Computer Systems Analyst. Born on October 17, 1941 in Detroit, Michigan, his parents were Valentine and Lena Mireles (both now deceased). Education: He received his B.A. in English Literature on June, 1968 at Wayne State University, Detroit, Michigan. In addition, he completed two years of post-degree studies also at Wayne State University. From 1960 to 1963 he worked as Personnel Specialist in the U.S. Air Force. He has also served as a U.S. Diplomatic Courier in the Foreign Service at the Frankfurt, Germany office from 1969 to 1970. More recently, he served as the Director of the Detroit based Latino Poets Association from October, 1988 to September, 1994. To date Gil has published over 170 of his poems. He has published two previous collections of his poems entitled, "Where Love Is," and "Colorful Impressions." Also, he has done many readings along with other members of the Latino Poets Association and he is familiar with being a performance poet. Gil's poems are usually short, concise with a lot of meaning and feeling. His ambition is to write poems of such quality that they will last for posterity.

Other Poetry books by Gil Saenz:

'Where Love Is'
2nd printing
Minnesota Ink, Inc., 1988
St. Paul, Minnesota

'Colorful Impressions'
Casa de Unidad Press, 1993
Detroit, Michigan

Anyone wishing to buy additional copies
of this book,
please call 1-800-247-6553.

($8.00 + $4.00 Shipping & Handling)

Quantity orders (orders of 5 or more) will receive
the book buyer's 50% discount.